UP CLOSE™

MONSTER TRUCKS

PAUL HARRISON

PowerKiDS
press.

New York

Published in 2008 by The Rosen Publishing Group
29 East 21st Street, New York, NY 10010

Author: Paul Harrison
Editor (new edition): Kate Overy
Editor (US edition): Kara Murray
Designer (new edition): Sylvie Rabbe

Picture credits: Alvey and Towers: page 14, top and bottom, page 20;
Andrew Fielder: front cover, title page, page 4, top and bottom; Monster
Photos: page 7, page 8, top and bottom, page 9, bottom right, page 10,
top and bottom, page 11, page 12, page 17, top, page 18, top and
bottom, page 22, page 24; Rex Features: page 16; page 21 photograph by
kind permission of Liebherr.

Library of Congress Cataloging-in-Publication Data

Harrison, Paul, 1969–
  Monster trucks / Paul Harrison.
     p. cm. — (Up close)
  Includes index.
  ISBN 978-1-4042-4223-4 (library binding)
  1. Monster trucks—Juvenile literature. I. Title. II. Series.
  TL230.15.H3685 2008
  796.7—dc22
                                                    2007033504

Manufactured in China

Contents

MEET THE

M onster trucks look like nothing else on the road. With their huge wheels and decorated cabs they look like normal trucks on steroids. But who first had the idea of making their truck look like that? And why? And what can these trucks do?

IN THE BEGINNING

The birth of the monster truck starts with a guy named Bob Chandler. In the early 1970s he began to customize his Ford pickup truck so it would work better when he took it off-road. He put on some extra large tires and soon Bob and his big truck were famous. It wasn't long before others started to follow his lead.

MONSTERS

BIG THREE

In the early days of monster trucks the make of truck you drove was quite important. The favorite manufacturers were Ford, Dodge, and Chevrolet. Each manufacturer had their supporters, and drivers seemed to be loyal to a specific brand. At times it seemed like a competition between these big three companies; so much so that manufacturers even sponsored some drivers.

RULES AND REGULATIONS

Monster trucks now compete against each other, and there's a whole range of rules and regulations that govern the sport. For example, the wheels can be no bigger than 66 inches (1.67 m) across, and there are certain types of fuel that monster trucks can't use, such as nitrous oxide. This is the fuel used by dragsters—imagine what a monster truck on this stuff would look like!

The governing body that regulates monster truck competitions is called the Monster Truck Racing Association.

BIGGER IS BETTER

The easiest way to make a big impression is to have the biggest wheels around. However, big wheels don't fit under the wheel arches of a normal truck, so the suspension of a monster truck needs to be jacked up to fit the wheels under, which in turn makes the trucks even taller. It looks great, but it makes the truck really tricky to get into—drivers have to climb the tires to reach some cabs!

TV TRUCKERS

Monster trucks are particularly popular in America, so much so that in 1993, the United States Hot Rod Association (USHRA) produced a television series called *Monster Wars*. On the show, monster trucks were modified to look like superheroes and given names such as Predator, Invader, and Grim Reaper. There were even *Monster Wars* toys and a video game!

GROWING POPULARITY

The USHRA now officially sanctions pro arena trucks, freestyle motocross, and all-terrain vehicle racing, but monster truck competitions frequently top the bill—and not just in America. Tournaments take place all over the world, from Canada to Sweden to Australia.

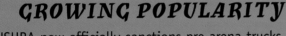

In addition to official racing events, there are also freestyle monster truck competitions. These involve jumping extra cars, vans, or caravans, which are piled up to make "pyramids."

UNDER THE SKIN

Monster trucks have come a long way from their humble pickup origins. Now they are expensive, state-of-the-art, custom-built machines specially designed to cope with their unusual tasks.

BODY SWAP

Although the truck bodies look like normal pickup trucks, they are in fact made out of one big piece of fiberglass. This means they can be molded into wacky shapes, but best of all they can be removed and replaced very easily when they get damaged—and this happens a lot. However, it also means that the doors on a monster truck don't open—they're just for show. The driver gets into the cab through a trapdoor in the floor of the truck!

CAGED IN

Monster trucks take a lot of punishment and this means the driver is at risk too. A series of strengthened bars, like a cage, stops the truck—and the driver—from getting crushed if the truck rolls over. Surely one of the few instances in which someone is happy to be behind bars!

WHAT A WHOPPER

Big trucks need big engines and they don't get much bigger than these. Monster trucks weigh around 10,000 pounds (4,500 kg) and can travel up to around 80 miles per hour (130 km/h) so they need large engines. What's more, they don't use normal gas or diesel either, but a special mix of alcohol and fuel for added performance.

TALL TIRES

A monster truck called Bigfoot 5 made it into *Guinness World Records* as the first monster truck designed to use 10 foot (3 m) tall tires—and nothing else. In 2002, it was crowned the world's biggest pickup truck.

SUSPENDED AUTOMATION

One of the biggest changes in the trucks is the suspension—the part that stops the ride from being too bumpy. When you're bouncing over cars or jumping through the air you want as soft a landing as possible. To prevent you from getting too many bruises on your backside these trucks don't have springs like normal cars, but gas-filled tubes, which work even better at absorbing bumps.

It's not just the front wheels that steer on a monster truck—the rear wheels turn too! This four-wheel steering is very handy for turning around in tight places.

9

CRUSHED

Monster trucks might look cool, but it was more than looks that made them famous. What they're really known for is the bad things they do to other vehicles and the distances they can jump.

ORIGINAL ATTRACTION

What really made monster trucks famous was their car-crushing ability. As the tires on the trucks got bigger and the suspensions got higher, their original purpose as off-road vehicles became a little redundant. People began to wonder what they could actually do instead. The answer was drive over wrecked cars. It sounded odd but was soon wildly popular, and if you've been stuck in a traffic jam before you can probably see the appeal of driving right over the top of it.

GOING UP, COMING DOWN

What could be more fun than driving over cars? How about taking off from a ramp and landing on them! It's a simple idea and a no-lose situation—a small jump means you land on the cars and the crowd is happy; go too far and it looks like a spectacular jump and the crowd is just as pleased!

RECORD BREAKERS

Once trucks began to take to the air it was only a matter of time before people were competing to see who could jump the farthest. Quite possibly the most remarkable jump to date was when Bigfoot 15 actually jumped over a 727 airliner. Normally it would be the plane you would expect to see flying, but Bigfoot trucks can do almost anything. The jump was a world record 202 feet (61.5 m). Another notable record was made by the truck Black Stallion. Although the jump measured only 70 feet (21 m), the driver was going backwards at the time!

The cars used in monster truck shows come from local scrap yards.

SAFETY FIRST

Trucks are often fitted with three kill switches, one on the back of the truck so the engine can be switched off in the event of a rollover, and the other two within easy reach of the driver. Drivers are required to wear helmets, safety harnesses, fire suits, and head and neck restraints. It's easy to see why!

PAINFUL

Big jumps take their toll on both the truck and its driver. Although monster trucks have massively improved suspension and safety cages, landing still plays havoc with their frames, often buckling suspension or trashing the fiberglass body. These are usually quite quick—if very expensive—to fix. The drivers are not so easy to repair. Injuries to a driver's spine are as common as damage to their kidneys.

Dennis Anderson, driver of Gravedigger 20, suffered a number of injuries during his racing years, including a broken kneecap, several broken ribs, a broken hand, and an injured wrist.

MUD
GLORIOUS MUD

Although smashing up old cars was a lot of fun for a while, even that got a little boring. A new challenge needed to be found. Mud bogging and sled pulling was the answer. Things were about to get messy.

MUCKY DEVILS

Mud racing, or mud bogging as it is sometimes known, is exactly what it sounds like—a sprint down a muddy track to a finish line. The trucks race two at a time, side by side down a 200 foot (61 m) long course—if they get that far. With those big wheels spinning through the mud you can guarantee that the dirt gets everywhere!

TRACTOR TROUBLE

Sled pulling was originally a competition between farmers and their tractors, so is often known as tractor pulling. Back then, to make the sled heavier people would jump onto it as it passed. Obviously this is a little dangerous, and as both tractors and trucks got more powerful, the sleds had to get heavier to make the vehicles work harder—so weights were used instead of people. That's good news for the people who don't have to risk life and limb jumping onto sleds, but bad news for the trucks as they've got to pull more weight.

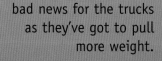

THE RIGHT MIX

Not just any old dirt will do at a mud bogging event. Organizers try to get the perfect mix of soil and water. If the mix is too dry, it's no challenge for the trucks; if it's too wet, the vehicles will sink as if in quicksand—funny for a while but what do you do when all the trucks have gone? There's an awful lot of mud to mix too, so diggers are used to do the job.

NO SNOW

If your idea of a sled is the thing you sit on to go down snowy hills you're in for a shock. These sleds are more like trailers with weights attached. The idea is to see how far the truck can drag the sled along a straight line course measuring 300 feet (100 m). The truck that gets the farthest is the winner. Of course it's not quite as simple as that. The weights on the sled move, so the farther the truck travels, the heavier the sled gets, making it even more difficult to pull. How cruel is that?!

If a truck hits the mud at the right speed it can sometimes zip across the top like a stone skimming across water.

15

FAMOUS TRUCKS

In the early days of monster trucks, it was their rarity that made them special and people would look out for them. However, when trucks started to compete against each other, they began to attract their own fans. This was split between people who liked an individual truck, and those who were loyal to the model of truck that the monster version was based on. Either way, the trucks became stars. Here are just some of the really famous ones.

BIG DADDY

Bigfoot is *the* monster truck—the first and the best. In fact there is more than one—every so often the truck gets upgraded to make it better than the one before. So far there have been 17 Bigfoot incarnations, and more than one runs at a time, so you've got plenty of chances to see them in action. There is even a Bigfoot that has tracks like a tank and is based on an army personnel carrier! With all these trucks, Team Bigfoot is the biggest and baddest on the planet!

MOLDED MONSTER

One of the benefits of using fiberglass bodies on trucks is that the molds can be made into any shape you like. This was the idea behind a famous truck called Samson. Named after the man from the Bible with superhuman strength, this truck looks like it has two huge arms extending from the cab. Samson's driver, Dan Patrick, might not look like that in real life, but at least his truck is a superstar.

GIRL POWER

Monster trucks might be mostly a man's world but there are some women out there who prove they're just as good at moving metal. One of the most well-known is Madusa. Already famous as a professional wrestler, Madusa turned to monster trucks in 2003 and already holds a couple of championships. That's one lady you don't want to mess with.

JUNKYARD GENIUS

When Dennis Anderson wanted to build a show-stopping truck he shopped where his budget allowed—the scrapyard. When other competitors laughed at him, he famously replied: "I'll take this old junk and dig your grave!" Anderson won the competition and earned his truck the nickname "Gravedigger." Today Gravedigger looks a lot different from the original version, but it remains as popular as ever and just goes to show what a bit of clever recycling can achieve.

PUTTIN' ON A

A monster truck show, or jamboree as they are sometimes called, is like no other show you'll see. No other sport can combine jumps, crashes, dirt and fire quite like a monster truck competition—and that's only the half of what you can expect to see!

LETTING RIP!

Unbelievably, racing, jumps, and crushing cars are not enough for some monster truck drivers—they want to show their artistic side, and they get their chance during the freestyle section of the show. This is the part where drivers can do what they like and go a bit crazy, performing doughnuts—that's spinning your car around in circles—and tire burnouts. This is when the back wheels spin really quickly but the truck doesn't move. It's noisy and smoky!

ROBOT MAYHEM

Cars get a pretty rough deal at truck jamborees. Sometimes they don't just get crushed by monster trucks, but they also get pulled apart by a different type of monster—a robotic one! Beasts such as Robosaurus can actually pick up cars and pull them apart with their teeth, as well as blast fire from their mouths. You don't get that at Formula One races! Awesome!

18

SHOW

Monster trucks are not deemed safe enough to travel on the roads and have to be transported in large trucks to each jamboree.

WARM UP ACTS

Although the monster trucks are the star attraction, there is usually some other motor mayhem for the crowd's enjoyment before the big act appears. This could be a bit of motocross racing—in which off-road bikes race around the track—or some stunt riding, or better still a demolition derby. This is when old beat-up trucks race around the track and smash into each other. It's pointless but fun!

SELL, SELL, SELL

A jamboree is also a good time for truck enthusiasts to get together and buy and sell stuff. Often you'll find stores selling everything from spare parts—so you can build your own monster truck—to hot dogs. There's also plenty of other stuff to do, from mini monster truck rides to inflatable castles—so there's lots to see before the real action takes place.

19

THE MONSTER

When people noticed the impact of monster trucks, they wanted their vehicles to get a slice of the action. As a result there's a range of machines that have been given the monster treatment.

MONSTER TRACTORS

Monster trucks may have borrowed sled pulling from the tractor world, but some tractors now look like monster trucks themselves. The tractors in the "unlimited modified tractor" class of pullers look like your average farm tractor on steroids. These are massive beasts and can weigh up to 8,000 pounds (3,600 kg). These tractors have some of the biggest engines you will ever see on land. Sometimes they have more than one!

At 15 feet 5 inches (4.7 m) high, Bigfoot 5 is the world's biggest monster truck. Its tires alone are 10 feet (3 m) tall.

FOUR WHEELS ARE BETTER

The first all-terrain vehicle, or ATV, was built in the 1970s. Early models had three wheels, but for stability this was increased to four; and the quad bike was born. There are now different sizes of quad bikes available and there are many quad bike racing events. However, they are still a useful off-road vehicle—in fact some farmers use them to round up sheep. You'd never be able to do that in a monster truck!

TREATMENT

MINI MARVELS

Ever wished you could be behind the wheel of a monster truck but can't since you're not old enough to drive? Well how about a mini monster that's remote-controlled! We're not talking about your little battery-operated toys here—these run on gas, diesel, and even nitro! They can travel at over 45 miles per hour (70 km/h) and can do amazing jumps. The trucks are so much fun they are sometimes the half-time entertainment at monster truck jamborees!

THE REAL MONSTERS

Believe it or not, there are vehicles out there that make monster trucks look like toy cars. The biggest trucks are those found in the mining industry—these machines have to move a lot of earth and rubble. The world's biggest is currently the Liebherr T 282 B, which stands at an incredible 24 feet 3 inches (7.4m) tall and weighs around 224 tons (203,000 kg). The cab is so far off the ground the driver needs to use ladders to climb into it!

GLOSSARY

BURNOUT (BURN-owt)
When a motor or electrical device breaks down because it has become overheated.

CUSTOMIZE (KUS-tuh-myz)
To build or change something to suit a particular person's needs.

FIBERGLASS (FY-ber-glas)
A strong material made from fine glass fibers, used for car bodies.

FREESTYLE (FREE-styl)
When a competitor is allowed to use whatever style he or she chooses, and the usual rules of the sport do not apply.

JAMBOREE (jam-buh-REE)
A large gathering involving speeches and entertainment.

MANUFACTURE (man-yuh-FAK-cher)
To make or produce something from raw materials.

MODIFY (MAH-dih-fy)
To change or adjust.

NITRO (NY-troh)
The name used to describe a specific chemical group.

NITROUS OXIDE (NY-trus OK-syd)
A colorless gas often used as an anaesthetic in dentistry.

SPONSOR (SPON-ser)
A person or organization that pays for an event, or the people involved in that event.

SUSPENSION (suh-SPENT-shun)
The springs that connect the wheels of a vehicle to its frame, designed to absorb shock and protect the driver.

TERRAIN (tuh-RAYN)
The surface texture of an area of land.

FURTHER READING

MONSTER TRUCKS (THE NEED FOR SPEED)
by Michael Johnstone
North Minneapolis, MN: First Avenue Editions, 2002

MONSTER TRUCKS (PULLAHEAD BOOKS)
by Kristine L. Nelson
Minneapolis: Lerner Publishing Group, 2002

MONSTER TRUCKS (500 SERIES)
by Scott Bryant
Lewiston, ME: Crestline, 2005

MONSTER TRUCKS (MIGHTY MOVERS)
by Sarah Tieck
Edina, MN: ABDO Publishing Group, 2005

MONSTER JAM: THE AMAZING GUIDE
by James Buckley
New York: DK Publishing, 2001

WEB SITES
Due to the changing nature of Internet links, PowerKids Press has developed an online list of Web sites related to this book. This site is updated regularly. Please use this link to access the list: www.powerkidslinks.com/upcl/montruck/

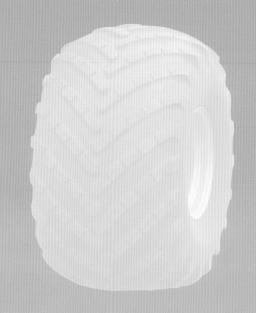

INDEX